WINTER ON AN AUTUMN DAY

Winter on an Autumn Day

Poems
by
DONNY BARILLA

Adelaide Books
New York / Lisbon
2019

WINTER ON AN AUTUMN DAY
Poems
By Donny Barilla

Copyright © by Donny Barilla
Cover design © 2019 Adelaide Books

Published by Adelaide Books, New York / Lisbon
adelaidebooks.org

Editor-in-Chief
Stevan V. Nikolic

All rights reserved. No part of this book may be reproduced in any manner whatsoever without written permission from the author except in the case of brief quotations embodied in critical articles and reviews.

For any information, please address Adelaide Books
at info@adelaidebooks.org
or write to:
Adelaide Books
244 Fifth Ave. Suite D27
New York, NY, 10001

ISBN: 978-1-951214-99-9

Printed in the United States of America

I rest in this rich, soft soil.
Early morning, the fog slithers,
I am surrounded in sweet mist.

Dedicated to, Gus Pappas

"Thank you."

Contents

Want 17
Vapors upon the Lake 18
Pollens Blooming 19
From Pond to the Scattered Garments 20
Slippery Leaves 21
Shrouded in the Dampened Leaves 22
Strings to an Instrument 23
Spring Passage 24
Stance of the Maple 25
A Day Spent Alone 26
Wild Scent 27
Perfect Rain 28
Hymns of the Rain Clotted Sky 29
Memorial Day, 2018 30
Glen and Grotto 31
Falling Winter 32
As the Geese Fly 33
Watching the Mist 34

Robes *35*
Arriving to the Summit *36*
Lighthouse *37*
Oak Leaf *38*
Feeding upon the Flickering Dew *39*
Apricot and Fig *40*
Ancestors *41*
Evergreen Mountain *42*
Bathing between Meadow and Creek *43*
Mountain Path *44*
Energy *45*
Facing East *46*
Invited *47*
Travel at End of Day *48*
Fading in the Woodlands Hour *49*
End of Day *50*
Evening Powders *51*
Breath *52*
Gazelle *53*
Lost in the Evergreens *54*
Earth *55*
Saps *56*
Bleeding Sky *57*
Dance *58*
Source of All Water *59*
Autumn Decay *60*
As Season's Shift *61*

Last Glance *62*
Reflections of Home *63*
Rain Hymnal *64*
Sleeping by Fields of Wheat *65*
Early Morning *66*
As the Moon Shifts *67*
By Night, By Day *68*
Morning Mist *69*
Grotto *70*
Hymns of a Woodland Night *71*
Woodlands Edge *72*
Upon the Down *73*
Lost in the Woods *74*
Glaze *75*
I Reach the Dancing Mist of Nightfall *76*
Recall in the Murmuring Woods *77*
Into the Sobbing Sky *78*
Storm *79*
Hiking from Valley and Hilltop *80*
Gathering Silks *81*
Dreams in the Deep of Night *82*
Altars and the Lavender Bush *83*
Wind against the Canvas *84*
Breath of You *85*
Pilgrimage *86*
Beneath the Sky *87*
Losing Her in the Mist *88*

Morning Awaits   *89*
Incense in the Chapel   *90*
Dreaming of Crows   *91*
Night's Shadow at the Shore   *92*
Funeral March at Twilight   *93*
Undressing beneath the Moonlight   *94*
Trail Leading Home   *95*
Finding the Forest Deep   *96*
Dreams from the Earth   *97*
Birch wood   *98*
As the Orchard Fades   *99*
Thickest Hour   *100*
Recollection by the River   *101*
Flickering Moonlight   *102*
Moans in the Field of Mist   *103*
Nocturne in the Woods   *104*
Across the Tumbling Ocean   *105*
Surrender to the Woods   *106*
Rest by the Fade of Maples   *107*
Trail of the Sun   *108*
Return to the Soil where I Sleep   *109*
Evening Walk   *110*
Waiting for Boats   *111*
Storm Spreads   *112*
Vapors Fade   *113*
Host at Close of Day   *114*
Winter's Sulk   *115*

WINTER ON AN AUTUMN DAY

Lost   *116*
Pampering Earth   *117*
Searching through the Forest Depth   *118*
Treasure   *119*
Cottons Fall   *120*
Ocean Cove   *121*
Winter Sets   *122*
Summer Glaze   *123*
Searching in the Woodlands   *124*
Soak   *125*
Rain Pastes upon the Field   *126*
Light begins to Fade   *127*
At the Pond   *128*
Pine Tree Forest and the Spring Water   *129*
The Days After   *130*
Permeate   *131*
Sweet Pastures   *132*
Swift Creek   *133*
Late Summer   *134*
Once   *135*
Fang   *136*
Far East   *137*
From Drought to the Fallen Rains   *138*
Fade   *139*
Deep of Autumn   *140*
Horizon   *141*
Stones and Mud   *142*

Tapping Rains *143*
Visitation *144*
She Comes from the Northern Mountain *145*
Mountain Trail *146*
House upon the Hill *147*
Open Gate *148*
Fumbling Weeds *149*
Swooning Verbs *150*
Lost into the Forest *151*
Adjacent to the Dash of the River *152*
Tamp of the Earth *153*
Fumbling Dust and Her Fading Flesh *154*
Fangs of Winter *155*
Oak Staff *156*
Tomb from the North *157*
Rejoice *158*
Requiem *159*
Lost in the Beams of Morning Light *160*
Woods *161*
Pulses at Morning *162*
Rain Day *163*
Tenderly I Walk *164*
Wax Pearl *165*
From Deep in the Woods *166*
Winter on an Autumn Day *167*
Dust *168*
Slumber *169*

Passage with the Pounding Rain   *170*
Shame beneath the Night's Sky   *171*
Bloods and Milks   *172*
Waltz beneath the Silver Moon   *173*
Jade   *174*
Host   *175*
Soils Fade   *176*
Trembling Dances   *177*
Earth Crumbles   *178*
Yoke of the Sky   *179*
Evergreen Woods   *180*
Searching through a Moaning Wood   *181*
Calendar of Youth   *182*
Walking in the Hour of Morning   *183*
Maps   *184*
Morning Rhythms   *185*
Oak Leaf   *186*
Fragments   *187*
Vacating   *188*
When Fog Falls   *189*
Wading before the Moon   *190*
Vanilla and Sandalwood   *191*
Awake in the Arms of Night   *192*
Drinking from the Mountain Spring   *193*
Velvets and the Bursting Pod   *194*
Warmth in Slumber as I Dream by Riverside   *195*
About the Author   *197*

Want

Triumph of the pines, stretch and settle as a crown,
peaked to the drip of the fog, born of a nestling groom,
pierced through the cones which fell in a dash.

Here, on mountaintop, the thinnest air cascades
across me in patterns and chip wood
nestles to the needle covered earth.

Several months later, I tread quietly through the valley.
Looking upon the stroke of the evergreen forest,
the slippery fog remains.

~

Now, by candlelight, I warm to the grooves and sauces
of warm Summer.

I hear the breath of the treetops rattle each branch and cone.

Standing from the breach of my window, I watch the clouds
soothe in a trembling fall as every whimper of grass

caresses me in want.

Vapors upon the Lake

Vapors cushioned the wave of this ancient lake.
Mist lulls me to a spirited sleep.

Into the clear of each trembling ripple and sweet
white capped rhythm, I grow upon you.

With the rains falling in early morning, I dance
in the moments of slumber and fall

To the grooves of each splashing wave.

By shoreline, I smell the brash, yet sweet aromas of water
upon moistened soil.

I tangle with the gloat of the moon as each tide
wrestles upon the sandy edge.

Then slowly, the cloud cloak the sky and all it's spread.

Pollens Blooming

I grew into the fibers of the jade colored meadow.
Pollens bloomed fresh against the late Spring hush.

I withheld my speech as the thicket, thorn bush and thistle
clung across my coat and patted my tender skin.

In the rise of the early morning sun, the palate
of the red, pink horizon flickered across me in lust.

The path, deepened and tamped to yellows,
washed through as the compass guiding.

I stopped for a moment, then continued.

From Pond to the Scattered Garments

Gathering light flooded to the hue of your chestnut hair;
flickering dance of each moon shadow
poised about the flesh of you as silver touch
brimmed across shoulders and stretch of the arms.

I softened to the strength of your fingers and palms.
I laughed into the burn of your lips.

~

Quietly the shoots of the bamboo shot for the cool sky,
heat rose from the humid press of the nearest pond
which licked the breeze in darting mist.

~

I left the poise of the wide stretch, heavy window.

Now, in the threads of Summer, I face
the garment covered floor.
I soothed across you, loud moans of
the rattling window which
crept about the room.

Slippery Leaves

Becoming aware of the stretch of your fingers
and the full cascade of your silk hair,
I cloaked, wrestled the comforter in a dance
to swell about you.

I looked upon the vast array of trembling trees.
I heard their moans which swept across the woods,
and soothed to the cry, flushing tears of the damest
dewdrops which settled in the arms of Spring.

I dreamt of the loosening leaf.

In covenant, I watched the branch croon with it's loss.

Along the slick passage of your sweaty, humid breast,
I fell across you as the leaves gathered
from pile to neighboring pile.

Shrouded in the Dampened Leaves

I followed the fragrance into the murmuring cove
which tossed waves of breathless air across me.

By water's edge, I traced my fingers long the whisper
of the grape hyacinth,

I filled my lungs with the laughing
weeds and tumbling treasures.

Sauced in the trellising rain, I trimmed
my ankles to the water's edge.
Silence fell across as the thrashing maples
spirited into the dance of each fumbling
molecule and dew driven
raindrop.

After the longest pause, I spoke to the
madness of the relentless
water.

In a moment later, I delved into the heavy forest
which shrouded me in dripping leaves.

Strings to an Instrument

My fingers fell across her as strings to an instrument.
Quietly, I soothed into the dance of each quivering moan.

I plucked upon the softest flesh from blanch of the thigh
to fevers threaded upon the scarlet pitch.

I opened my mouth and grew thick in the discovery
of the dampest slip of the dampest bead.

Quaking across the hems of this comforter and gown,
I wrestled my way to the salts as flickering to the breasts,
alive in each drizzle of silent creams.

Spring Passage

The delicate frost melds to the soft soils
resting by the spread of the blooming tree.

I hear the crisp slap of the branches as they scurry
from green bud to warming fevers of coming Spring.

As I look upon the quiet powders of your freckled chest,
a single snap of a single twig falls to the patterned earth.

I gather the sneering bud, caked in molds of mud,
and listen to the whistle of white falling to browns and tans.

By the hour of late evening, I walk to the woods
and tamp the press of my feet,
so sweetly I think of you.

You will return to me upon a Summer breeze.

Stance of the Maple

I look upon the temperance of the vast, heavy forest,
stretching across the thick, rolling hills.

I smell the maple, I smell the pine and spruce.

Sulking, slow drift of the mountain creek
digs through the silent earth and settles upon the lake
dampened and humid in the perch of the valley.

Swift, I drink and ease the sweat from
my temples and cheeks.
In the dance of a moment,
I swell and walk across the mulch and rising aroma
of the awakening earth which clutters
through the gathering trees,
flickers each twig and leaf.

The seeping pulp of the sap,
burrowed deep in the regal stance of the maple,
I gather a fallen leaf and crumble it in the palm
of my pinching hand.

Dust takes to the frolicking wind.

A Day Spent Alone

Against the fractured brim of dawn,
clusters of the creamiest yellows gather with the softest blues.

Silently, by the end of day, buds open and fill
my searching lungs with their scent.

I cross the hushing, breeding croon of the maddened
meadow as the pod smack against each other

and unravel with the flickering leaves, still
calm as the skies refrain.

There lives a sulking posture of the eager mass
of the oak tree which stands open and entirely alone.

Now in the deep of evening,
I rest and ponder the depth of this soil
which tugs upon the stance of my haunches.

Clouds fade as the purples begin to swell,
I ease my sight to the fluttering pink
which weaves through the slender bloom of the horizon.

Wild Scent

The air hung damp as each drizzle upon the wavering ferns
gripped the moisture and tugged it to the earth.

Heavily, the forest's scent wrapped across me.

In an feverish spread, I wandered lost,
yet soon found by the slice of the freshest stream.

I followed this remark into the mountain which gleamed
to the cloudy thresh as each riveting rock punctured the sky.

Dripping in the wild scents, I edged the step of my boot
and found my way home.

Perfect Rain

Silks of her dress fell about the forest floor.
I collected them as leaves brushing
through my calloused hands.

With a measured gust of wind,
I turned to the west and watched as the sun,
cluttered in ribbons of light,
faded to the crackling snicker of neighboring trees.

Each thread unravelled and the warmth
of this late Spring night
fell to a crisp dance
which tangled me in ginger touch.

I watched as the belly of the sky flooded us in perfect rain.

Hymns of the Rain Clotted Sky

I dredged through the milks, foams
she bore in her tender pouch.

The finch, sparrow, and the lark trembled
their way across the patio hunting for seeds.

Burrowing through the garments she wore,
scattered as the morning light which
flickered through the bedroom
window. I flooded her in silent graze and touch.

The sky sliced open and fumbled a haze of misty rain.
I spread open my mouth and gathered each drop
soothingly in the goblet of my mouth.

Swiftly, sauces of the morning drizzle
pasted to the thin cottons of her shirt.

~

Into the groan of the now scorching, torn open sky,
I walked the grotto in measure of the winded red maple
which thrashed about in chymes and sang sweet
hymns to the vanished birds.

~

Pleasantly, I wrapped full about her mouth.

Memorial Day, 2018

I hear you through the misty vapors
of the stillness of the glen.
I open myself to your blooming moans.

Moments later, I kneel to the earth and
stroke the silks of your flickering hair.
Against the soils upon my pressing fingers,
I absorb to your breath.

Glen and Grotto

Pearls, trembling white, perch upon the
creak of the old pine wood
porch, suspending to the threads of passing air,
opening as a breath against the tapping rain.

I sit calmly in this haze of soft nurture.

The mountains to the south sulk in the approaching fog.
I lean my gaze to the spread of a dew driven lawn.
The clusters of Spring flowers laugh to the breeze.

Nearby, the elm trees host a splash of the greenest moss.
Each grass blade speaks silently to the lick
of the soothing mist, alive in this measurement of patience.

I drip my softened feet through the glen and grotto.

Falling Winter

These mountains, filled with trees, empty themselves
of an endless gown of leaves.

Yellows, tans and browns flood the pine floor,
quietly spread with needles.

Now thrust into the masks of the palest Winter,
powders sulk as the birch wood claims kingship.

~

As the days pass, I watch the alabaster mounds
gather from base to peak.

~

In the freshest moment, the crows fleck in spots of black,
threading across the pools of snow.

I breath the icy air and gesture home as I reach
the trail which guide me home.

As the Geese Fly

The robins trample swift upon the winds.
The geese veer their way south as the blind sky
opens as a canvas.

Fallen leaves powder to mulch, paused upon
each tap of the settling mist.

Miles away, I hear the screaming torrents of Winter
attack in their voidless shape.

I turn to the pine trees, sitting, sulking, and soothing.
Chills tangle across my spine as I hide
in these trembling woods.

Watching the Mist

The misty rain gathered across the flickering
waves of the flooding lake.

I filled my lungs, throat and mouth
with the scents of the bordering wild flowers,

Taunting the stretch of the deepened soils
which proclaim of their fragrant mulch.

In the breath of morning,
fog whisps across the sleek, rippling caps.

By nightfall, the fattened pulse of the moon,
riddled in rings, fastens in silver slivers upon the tender water.

Robes

Standing before the open timber gates
which hung as a path to the northern mountain,
I walked upon the fresh dewy earth, filled
with pressed gathering leaves, drenched open
as the breath of this forest grooms and pats.

I hear the crackling mesh of the branches.
I fill my mouth with scented breath;
the mint leaves slept across this narrow path.

Hearing the moans of this early summer dance,
I look the the sky and declare my witness
as the migrating birds slice through both clouds
and the trembling blouse of this fallen sky.

The maple, regal in all the majestic
spread of it's towering gown,
robes me in sweet saps from limb to trunk.

Arriving to the Summit

The mountain trail burrowed jagged with rocky teeth
snapping through the clay earth and crusted depth
of each nearby tree.

I paused upon a heavy stone and flung my sight
to the pass of the thin cotton clouds.

I slipped my fingers through the tossing leaves
and I could smell the vast years of the churning earth.

~

She once walked this path, fastened to the chymes
of spreading seasons, opening her pale white flesh
to each press and tug of the wind and all it's ginger touch.

Looking north to the mountain peak,
the fog depressed and I heard the faintest moan
flex across the summit.

I smelled, felt her fragrant spices in the blooming breeze.

Lighthouse

With treasured patience, I wait, stand
by the nearest lighthouse.

Fog slithers across as the waves smack
their foamed white caps

against the gnarled heavy stones.

Walking the edge of the water, I hear the seagulls

as they moan their way through the swift, tender mist.

I wait for her fullness to thread it's way across me,

soothe each speck of rain to sauce through
the madness of my flesh.

Boats slice their way, dancing through the fog which creeps

as a voice through the slithering waves.

I turn and face my way to the sweet
rise of her trembling breasts.

Quick, she engulfs me into the most distant region.

I walk to her and meet her upon the smoothest sands.

Oak Leaf

I study the giggling of the slight of the passing creek.
gently, slowly, a single oak leaf floats downstream.

Beyond, in the plush verbs of the spread of the meadow,
the hickory tree fumbles with the breath, stroking past.

Here, the depth of the earth sulks, packs with the most
fertile minerals.

~

I hear the rains swab through the gray low hanging clouds.

A few hours past, the creek swelled as the soil moans
with the most excitable pleasure.

I listen to the winds rattle the fumbling branches.

Feeding upon the Flickering Dew

These bones, served in the richness
of the dusty, tumbling dirt,
moan in a sweetened pitch where soil softens and rejoices.

My feet stepped upon you as sweet passages, tender voices
triumphed through the crumbling leaf and moss.

I look to the horizon and pale yellows
partnered with slippery pinks
proclaim of your surrender and travel from molecule to beads
of the pearl white flickering dew.

I lift the leaf. I place a touch of water upon my tongue.
Listening, tasting, you burrow through the tangs
of my mouth as each whimper of your
voice thrashes about me.

To be the subject of the soil and rains,
I fasten myself to the throne upon the
earth which crawls about me
in the fevers of earth and all it's tender fugues.

Apricot and Fig

She tugged her gown, tossed the satin touch
of her garment, exposing the vulnerable twitch
of her breasts and abdomen, the fullness of her thighs
as she melded the fluttering pulse of her chest
against the spread of my trembling hands.

By morning, the fog wrapped across the wooden planks
of the home.

Her sweet scent and spice of her silky hair
swabbed across me.

I heard the morning birds as they perched and sang.

I posed, looked and glanced upon the burrow of her stitch.
Moments later, the sweeping broom of the sundance,
all it's rays, climbed our flesh as the ripe wish
of the apricot and fig.

Ancestors

Into the rain, pearls drift upon the wind, I stand
motionless as the dash of morning light
soothes and drenches upon me.

In the drip of nightfall, the low slouching moon
caressing with silver rings as the trees I stand near
groom upon the dancing breath of early Summer.

I feel the humid touch gather about my neck
and fasten on the wash of my hair.

Now as the breath of morning tugs me to the spirits,
minerals, and mulches, I resume the crouch
of my ancestors and the bones of them which
welcome my tender flesh.

Evergreen Mountain

The falling leaves crawled across my shoulders
and clung to the shirt dampened to my back.

My flesh absorbed the scent of Autumn.
My lungs, once filled with sweet fragrance,
depleted to the moans of the earth.

I rattled my bones to the rocks and pebbles
which sulked and tremored in this soft soil.

As a dancing carpet of lint, fresh from the dying trees,
I offer my dusty lint upon every slapping wind,
brooming trees and their crazed branches.

Into the height of the evergreen covered mountain,
thickly spread to the north, I offer my breath
with each tug of the passing clouds.

Here I slumber in the voice of each breeze
and splash of the rumbling heavens.

Bathing between Meadow and Creek

I bathe in the tremors of early morning
as the light glances through the trees,
flickering upon every puzzling leaf.

Nearby, the slice of the prowling creek
gushes down the hillside and softens
the closeness of a sunken meadow.

The sweet scents of jasmine fill me
in the treasure of this tumbling wind,
tender upon this mask of early day.

I soothe with the touch of the pollens
and their candied breath.

I send the swift broom of my spreading fingers
across each shrub and withering sprout.

Mountain Path

I stand upon the clay of the earth,
softly I moan as the bones rattle and murmur.

Sweetly, I taste the marrow cross across the tender breeze.
I wrap myself in these lowering, thin clouds.

Below, I watch as the meadow waves and tangles
with the breath of the sloping sky.

In the tastes of this morning, I sulk and weave
my way through the mountain path which strokes

The summit much in the way I touch the creams
of your neck and breasts.

The day proceeds much in the way each molecule
rattles throughout the flesh of me.

I touch the powders of this caked and crusted earth.
wandering, the girth of the occasional pine woods

I felt the much awaited soothing press of dampness
and soft moisture tapping upon my eager skin.

Energy

Into the gasp of the wind, the oak leaves trembled
and dove across the grassy pouch which held
the stem and the crumble of the fading edge.

Gathering a few, placing them in the cup of my hand,
I waited as the dust flew upon the thin film of weathered
air. Fine and crumbled, the scent of the dying earth

filled the pleasant touch upon my face.

I roamed the endless meadows, pastures and fields.
Wilting grass, tans, browns of the stalk
crunched beneath my feet.

I entered the press of the richest soil.
I stay still as the energy of the earth ripens across me.

Murmuring a stroke of the tender voice, I listen
to the dance of the eager silks, threading
through the quiet breath
of the shaking, wilting trees.

Facing East

The glaze of the frosted pine quakes to the frozen wind
which trellises across the southern hills.

Becoming the chant of morning, I hear the brooming
snow driven dust bury in the sloping mounds.

Slowly, I turn my burning face to the east,
so softly, the I absorb the rise of the sun.

Pangs of a warmer day brings stings to the hidden
foot of the soak, spread across my boots.

I walk the path to the endless slash of the sun
always rising, how I am facing east.

Invited

The forest sent soothing breath upon the tremble
of the pine tops and sap of the most gentle maple.

The air grew warm as the ferns wiggled to the press
of the frolicking wind.

The moss offered rest to the patterns of each north
graze and fever of the shaking mulch.

Quiet, I walked into the lush greens and maps, brown,
upon the stretch of the tree.

"Please rest. Surrender to all I offer within these fastened
woods. I grow in the mulch of the voice of my ancestors.
rest tender."

"I rest by mountain spring and drink deeply
as the waters gush across me."

Travel at End of Day

Sulking branches, I sit covered in leaves as threads
Of silk rest upon my neck and head.

Powders, pollens from the bursting pod,
Enrich the cool, stillness of my flesh.

By evening, I feel myself tear in a slice,
A flash of treasure which deepens into the soft earth.

I return to you in dusts upon a breath
From the crown of the stance where the mountain rests.

The gravity of these atoms return to the patterns
From which they came.

I look upon the gesture of the empty trees,
Once holding leaves, now boasting of their nakedness.

I fall, empty of life and drift upon the throat
Of this passing stream and dampen in the path

Which leads to the open, endless sea.

By nightfall, I wrap myself in salts and sands.

Fading in the Woodlands Hour

Clusters of fumbling leaves broom along the forest floor,
neighboring trees with roaming, spreading moss
set so still for the crimping leaves, take upon the wind.

I angle my face to the flickering sunlight which
relishes through each wrestle of the branches
as they glint upon these muffling sounds of Autumn.

The naked haunch of my feet
bury through the dirt which sings the psalms
of ancestors and fragments upon the breeze.

I feel the pulse of the nearby, spirited river.
for a long moment, I kneel to the white capped rippling
gush of spreading water.

Of all the nestling scents, of all the shrouded woodlands,
here, I return to the gloat of the temple,
canopied canvas, arching trees.

End of Day

Fine dust, pollens, and bursting pods
sweep through the meadow and open as a gown
lulling upon the sweet flowers in the wind.

I dip my fingers to each shoot and sprout.
I wallow in the voice of the trembling grasses.

~

The sap of the maple tree longs for the tip
of my tongue and the roof of my saturated mouth.

~

Now, the end of day, I walk alone, yet
feel the lush wheats as they undress against me.

~

I walk the endless trails.
I whimper songs to the bristling breeze.

Evening Powders

From her beauty, gales slipped across her slick, moist tongue.
In the fullness of my silk hair, her breath motioned
my crown, bustling in each: west, east, south, and north.

By the shadow of nightfall, I placed my lips
sweetly upon her breasts, alive in all their nakedness.

Evening powders rose from the tuck and bend
of the earth. I found her in the clay mounds of the soil.

With the croon of each dancing wind,
I hold forever in the goblet
sunk sweetly my jaw. Her passions rose in the honeys
which sulk through each tender hive.

I press my body against the dusty memories of her.
I station upon the gravel and tender mulch.

Breath

I gathered myself into the fullness of this mountain's breath,
scathed across the boulder and shredding the tender stream.

Turning to the depth of nightfall,
I mourned the loss of each passage leading home.

Fibers from the crumbled leaves scattered across me.
Aromas of the pine woods soothed near;

I dipped my mouth to the trembling
ripples of the deep blue stream.
Swallowing as blades dripping down my heavy throat,

the fog began to lift.
I swiftly turned and placed myself on the path
which unveiled the motions leading home.

Gazelle

Into the majestic flowery scent of her neck,
I reached upon her as a cool, smothering lake
which touched in the smallest of ripples
and slithered along the quietest of shores.

With the most eager of motions,
I moved the milks from her pouches, breasts.

Kelp wrestled about her calves and feet.
I lulled to the calm of her nape and nave.

Sitting calmly, quietly I watched as the gazelle
darted through the reaching trees, alive in the press
of hoof to fern.

Now, the fullness, heavy bloom of the silver moon,
scattered upon us. In radiance, her nakedness tamped
upon me; I swelled about her in the fattening thickness
of an eager foggy mist, risin to the canopy of the heavy trees.

I slept upon the quivering satchel of her abdomen.
I knelt beside her and quaked
as the rising moon swathed us in gentle hues

Lost in the Evergreens

I loosened through the garments which
hung as mist upon the forest floor.
Each branch, alive and moaning, slept
through tender motions.

Bark of the evergreen swelled about the glances of my face.
Softly, this generous flesh, gathered every perching bead
of moisture and groaning sweat.

I lofted to the path which lead me to you.
I poised to the path which tore me from you.

After walking endlessly, I found you in the meadow.
I touched you as the strength of the wind
lessened our grooming hands.
By morning, I walked with the sun
gnawing upon my back, neck.

Earth

My voice threw upon you as each branch of the willow tree
crumbled in dust, settling upon the earth.

Clouds, fattened in the forest, dispersed.
I left this place in clarity and surmounting answers.

You thrived against my neck and chilled
each patch of Winters early arrival, blooming white.

I hear the gnarled rattle of the pine woods.
I watch as the oak declares every pronunciation
to the wind which scours from the north.

In the marvel of this end, I sweeten to
the pasture, glen, and meadow,
this place I gently belong.

I feel the mosses stretch across me as I fade in this arena
of landing leaves and smack of each branch.

Saps

Autumn flecks burrow in her damp, moist eyes.
I feel the winds of early November as I brood upon
these sauces which swab across me and open my tender flesh.

I gather upon the breath of this cool evening.
I watch as my fine hair flickers across temple and spine.

Now, in the girth of night, I watch you as you flash
upon the moon slowly surpassing the cotton clouds
which flood the horizon, patterned gauze.

Your lips wrap as ice upon the pine tree.
I touch the frozen saps as the depth of night tumbles past.

Bleeding Sky

The Autumn leaves scattered along the bending stream.
Upon the breath of the lifting clouds,
I waded through each channel.

Lone. The crow wavered on the spruce,
bending branch against the breeze.

South mountain, in the distance, clung to the vapors
on ridge and summit.

I waited until Spring and watched the prisms dance upon
the approaching fractures of dawn.

Plunging, each mountain spring fed the valleys in girth
and width. I felt these sauces soak the to the softest soil.

Quick. The crow takes to the air and deepens
with fluttering wings as the trembling
breath of the mountainside
offers and shakes the spreading roots of this heavy soil.

I soak in these colors of tan, brown, red, and yellow.
the sky bleeds upon me.

Dance

He dances through the hustling winds.
Open upon the tremors of a most silent earth,
the sun gloats of his touch and burning neck.

He wades through the fullness of the trembling
sash of morning. The earth pulses along the rhythms
of each foot and groan of the calf.

By midday, the crumbling leaves saunter,
the branches rattle in homage of the
muscling ferns and weeds.

Source of All Water

I open to the endless roaming tongue of the east.
Endless sun quivers upon my burnt, squinting face.

I walk upon the dusts and clays of the meadow,
alive in grasses and moaning shoots of the climbing bamboo.

I search for the source of all water.
I search for the tremble of every stream and puckering gush
of the sweetest spring.

With nightfall ceased, I follow the creek and stream.
Tender, the sun splashes upon me in the heaviest flood.

~

I awaken to the sky masked in marmalades
and dripping in yellows.

I stand to the shaking window and watch a single leaf
travel the coursing brook.

With the heaviest of all temptations, I sulk in the meadow,
dredging in floods.

Autumn Decay

I curl beneath the auburn sky,
flooding lights of Autumn stretched across me
as did the fading, crumbling leaves
which scattered along the edges of my body and face.

Hooked, my toes burrowed through the crimping ferns
and slouch of the most tender moss.

I hear the anguish of approaching Winter.
The treetops rattled in madness.

This forest sulks as a grave filled with fading pulses.

Spearing winds slash across me.
I fill the soils in chills and glosses
of the coming dancing powders
which reach for the pounding glen.

Here, flickering grasses and ices grooming upon
the earth, meadows clash with the tumbling woodlands,
branch to branch and chiseled acorn upon bedded leaves.

As Season's Shift

I listen to the whisper of the budding leaf.
Pine saps perch upon bark and stem as I
thread my way through the timber, softly bedded forest.

Looking to the treetops, arching branches, light flickers
through in a dazzling dance.

I sit in the stillness of a quiet posture
and soothe my face to the breath of
elm, maple and sycamore.

As nightfall arrives, I stand and hunt the trails which
pattern the woodland floor.

At last, I tremble through the chill of the passing stream.
Beneath the sauntering waters, in the channel deep
I dip through the current as I feel my hair bloom
upon the chiseling draft.

I beg upon the chill of the throttling breeze.
I dredge my lungs to the fullness of spice and drifting aroma.

I can sense the moistures gather in the shadowy sky.

Last Glance

I bring myself to the edge of her painted lips;
she unfolds herself as the winds upon a groomed meadow.

I unleash the pouches of her breasts,
together we wrap among the foams;
we hear the distant sands gathering milks of the ocean deep.

The freckles of her bust and fullness of her torso
gather as the diamonds, beads of the tender night's sky.

Pleasant agony of the pulsing groin;
I hear the lusty seagulls and the dancing grasses.
I witness the bend of her waist and trembling thighs.

I wade into the darkness of night.
Turning behind, I watch the fading peach hues of your skin.

I stop to gather a bead of dew and place
it on the edge of my tongue.

Reflections of Home

I can feel the earth breathe, unveil
as the blouse wrangling upon the hardwood floor.

Meadow after meadow, I gather the scents of the patches
of mint which surrender to my pulsing lungs.

I walk my way to the western winds of the fragrant forest.

Each jade colored bud stretches for perching moisture.
The crest of my boots dampen as I surf through the wet
flickering plant and yearning shrub.

Thinking of you and all your chiseled nakedness,
I follow the trail leading home.

Rain Hymnal

The sky screamed in preludes as the sobbing glens
filled midnight with rivets, marinating the nocturnal breath
with sweet trembling water.

I stand beneath the slouching eaves.
Rain gathers before me.

I hear the depth of this heavy night open in hymns,
gushing breezes open as a choir.

I send my sight through the rattle of the orchard.
Apples crouch beneath the reaching arms as leaves flicker.

I return to my home and rest by the shreds of candlelight.
Gingerly I lull to the slapping rain.

Sleeping by Fields of Wheat

I thread my fingers through the locks
of your walnut colored hair.
Among the peaks and valleys of the silk bed,
the feathers of the down pillow perch
against our heads and necks.

I touch with the tremble of your thigh,
I softly edge through your fields of wheat.

As the glimpse of morning sun shatters through the window,
I sleep in the fracture of this heavy grip of dawn.

Fading, I can hear the breath beneath your breasts
fill the dust covered room.

Early Morning

I edge my way from creek to stream as tufts
rise, the grass and the onion sprouts.

In the dance of a moment, rain taps as a spread,
thick, the skies swell and envelope a humid press.

Quick glance, the geese stab across the ash gray sky.

I open my mouth and feel the trickling mist.

~

Into the position of the stretching dash of streams
plunging, blossoming waters fill the lake.

~

I relish in the haze and dark mask of
the earliest morning hour.
With the mulch's scent rising to the treetops,
I breath the plunging flood of the darkening sky.

As the Moon Shifts

The tumbling creek basted the rocky ledge,
I smelled the cloak of Spring.

Moss spread to the haunch of the nearest tree.
Reaching from prowling root to base and lift of the trunk.

The sweet moisture deepening from the sky
filled the breath of my tongue, lungs.

By midday, I returned to the pasture.
Gently, I slept beneath the great oak
which tangled upon the breeze.

Soft, the soil lay by my slumbering body.
I rest upon the glance of the fading moon.

By Night, By Day

I sink beneath the sun,
I dance beneath the moon.

Navies of the moaning sky pulse
through the midnight breath.
Sweetly, you dampen to the fields of grass.

I watch the cloth you wear,
fall as the maple leaf, clutter upon the earth,
the blouse you shed.

Sulking, sinking clouds wrap across the breasts you feed
to the moaning stretch of the earth.

By morning, you dissolve with the rise of the sun.

I retreat to the forests which tug upon the fertile hills.

Morning Mist

I slithered across you as ferns across the forest floor;
Dancing fingers tug through the the
open breath of flickering air.

The haze, dripping fog kissed upon the tender soil.
I reach for you as you pass my touch with withering silks.

I lay my flesh with nakedness of the
sulking yeasts of the earth.
Open fields whisper to me.

Wavering mist croons upon my tender face.
I turn in all directions as the earth and soothing winds retreat
To the facets of the mornings rising sun.

Grotto

Your breath bloomed across me.
I fell to the twitch of your pale, fumbling thighs.

The touch of your thin parted lips
pressed me across the warm winds of Summer's edge.

I dance with the fragrance of the fullness
of your sauntering hair,
cloaked the hue of chestnuts;
I lost my way with the auburn sting of your clever eyes.

~

Walking with you in the fresh spices of your tender grotto,
I sank beneath you.

I looked upon the crescent moon.
Sweetly, I tugged the curve of your bending waist.

With morning near, the fog sulked as the smoky breath
of quiet glazes touching the spread
of each patch of wild grass.

Hymns of a Woodland Night

Among the thrashing beard of the heavy stroke of Winter,
I walked into the deep of the whitest woods.

Looking across the pine and all it's sulking cones,
the maple chanted in the softest hymns.

Foggy mists stretched across the canvas of the treetops.
I begged for it's silky touch.

As the tamp of my boot deepens
through the grazing powders,
I think clearly of the acorn and the snap
of the stick, thrown asunder.

Roaming in the deepest hour of night,
the wind scurries the bark as every tree moans to the wind.

I listen to the breath of night.

Woodlands Edge

I watch the dance of the feathering wind
lather among the leaves as they take to the sky,
land across the gentle touch of the gentle hills.

I wade through this.
Waist deep the dying crimp of the moaning crunch
as my legs brush each aside.

I hear the screams of the distant forest.
Adjusting, I reach the woodlands edge.

Upon the Down

I soothe through the shifting dance of the ash gray fleece.
From pouch to garment the moisture roams
and floods each bend and snip.

The down your tender head rests upon
softens and sweats the floods of my chestnut hair.

I saunter with the tremble of your quivering abdomen.
I hear the sea in every slick bead of sweat.

Into the madness of this early Summer night,
the flooding gates pinch with every glaze.

Into the distance, I hear the sheppard
tend each flock of wool.

Swift, I roam into the salty streaming dew;
alive the moans of this spirited warmth creep beneath me.

Lost in the Woods

With the twist of the wind,
I taste the mint which nestles in the roaming grotto.

With naked legs and naked feet,
I search for her as the gray clouds spread across
the curve of the moon.

Along the edge of the thick of the weeds,
I dampen through them as flesh to a spear.

Here, the garden meets the fondling, sulking sash
of the moaning forest.

From gnarled branch to wilting leaves,
the choir of the crimping twigs step upon the floor;
I can hear the wind laugh through the treetops.

Soon, I am lost.

Glaze

My leaning face upon the pulse of your veins,
we lull to the gushing creek.

Your powdered neck soothes as the dripping
fog grazes beneath the heavy horizon.

~

Miles I walk as the grasses snap beneath my feet.

The Autumn sun glazes with the Autumn moon.

~

Into the deep of the wild, your scents fall upon me.

I Reach the Dancing Mist of Nightfall

As I stand upon the thick jade of the stretching meadow,
I watched the purples and navies drip in tangling mist.

Nightfall shrouds across me,
I coil in the heavy sauces of late evening;
warm rain taps along the tamped traces of my pausing boot.

~

I think back to the blazing sun.
I roam across the silks of your bloomed, full, dampened hair.

The trees relish in the blushing wind.

Miles at a distance, I searched for nightfall
as the scents you groom dance from the soaking meadow.

~

I found you in the trance of the endlessly thriving stream.
I filled the deep pouch of this goblet and suckled my way
to the grassy sprouts where you lay and rest.

Recall in the Murmuring Woods

I cross the gray pebbled road.
Into the depth, from limb to twig, from leaf to dancing fern,
I find an obscure light which flutters through the towering treetops.

I smell the smoke of each campfire and it's snarling wood.

Faintly, I hear the rippling, lavish spread of the pooling creek.
I steer my eyes upon the moist, rich earth
and hear the moans we shared past Fall.

Into the Sobbing Sky

I absorb you in the fragrance bloomed
upon this pillow's down.
I fall across you as the rippling white gush of the stream.

With the pulsing sun strapped along
the burn of my tender neck,
I swoon to you in passing mist.

I quiver to the dampness dripping from the thin lips
you press, then pause, then press again.

I see the tender blanched clouds rise in dissipation,
then sulk again.

Along your pleasant trail,
I snip the rose and loosen the petals into the sobbing sky.

Storm

Drums throbbed their quavering gush
across the heavy stream.
Pasted in rains, I look to the sky which slivered as a gash;
scowling winds moaned through the nakedness of night.

The smack of the spirited droplets cupped and dripped
from each vein of the tender leaf.

I rose my face to the slaughter of the sky which
drew sauces along every nook of tree trunks
and stretch of root.

By the thick warmth of morning, I stood and wrestled
my way through the thicket and shrub.

Softly, the mud begged for me.

Hiking from Valley and Hilltop

The pine wood stretched the curving hills.
I softened above the scattered needles;
crows darted from limb to the piercing treetops.

Here, in the valleys slouch,
the stiff grassy tufts of the peppered earth, stone and pebble,
rose by late Summer in the thread of a spear,
jousting the naked sky.

I paused and placed a wooden nut in the pouch
of my barren mouth.

Upon the mountaintop, I look back and my trembling eyes
lulled the dampness of the heavy valley
which opened as a meadow, forever fertile.

Gathering Silks

From the breeze lofting across the moistened fields,
I rest my torso and bust upon the
treasures of the tangled wheat.

I angle my sight to the sleek breasts you undress and soothe
to the tread of my slight, thin parted lips.

We gather the silks of the tempered earth.

Softly, you walk into a distance as I relish in the pampering
crimping gown you so sweetly leave behind.

From wind and the breath of morning, I hear you as
the wheats part and gather each bead of shattered dew.

Dreams in the Deep of Night

Into the grave of your tepid mouth,
the humid press of your tongue,
I roam your galaxy as the sweat pearls upon the supple
poise of your neck, temples.

Softly, I absorb the powdery fragrance of your
warm breasts which begin cooling at the stretch of nightfall
and all it's trellising ribbons,
colored the deepest navies.

I saute across you as the sweet scents of the earth
rise to the flex of flesh and darting glances.

By evenings end, you bloom the endless sky
with each tear roaming the fragrance of my heavy neck.

In the flash of a lucid awakening,
I wake to the empty sounds of an empty flourished home.

Altars and the Lavender Bush

I gazed upon her as she swam in the cool trembling lake.
Beneath the surface, her chestnut silk hair bloomed
full as the wavering breath which would pull across
distant peak mountains and chisel through the well
spread and scattered pines.

The naked lush pull of her chilled flesh
opened her body as an altar.

Gushing foams writhed upon the pebbled shore.
She broke the film for a proud sauntering gasp of air;
water flooded the curves of her nudity.

~

A year later, I walk the empty shoreline.
For a second, I smelled the distant lavender
as it stroked it's way across the mourn of the
lake.Altars and the Lavender Bush

Wind against the Canvas

The sap pulled through the soft touch of the wood.
Softly, I lean my head and neck against the sweet shade
of the maple which fluttered breath against my hair and ears.

I looked to the treetop and discovered the sun
as it tore through the dancing leaves.

I placed the stem of the leaf into the palm
of my hand.

Upon gathering my things, I walked through the grotto.
Wind soothed as a canvas;
I found a nutshell and continued forth.

Breath of You

Against the spread of the sun,
I watched you turn and face east as the flicker of dust
gathered about you, resting upon shoulders
and your pale trembling arms.

The scent of you drifted swift into my lungs.
I challenge you along the moisture perching,
grass amd thick of the moss.

Placing the cup of my palms along the ribs
of your shivering torso,

I open you to the breath of this wild meadow.

I stop briefly, pluck a petal of the thickest flower,
we scatter across the wind.

Pilgrimage

I follow the path riddled in stones
and branches thrown askew.
Here, your trace, wallowing scents grip me
as I kneel to taste the crisp gushing spring.

From above the trees,
I hear the rattling moans of you fading voice
as I grip the sapling and turn my face
to the ash colored moon.

I feel your breath upon my lips.
Engaging the undergrowth where you lay
years ago,
I climb the summit we once climbed.

I fall to the sweet fragrance of the tender mint leaves.

Into this passage of night's cloaking gown,
I curled and slept as the cottons of fog
emptied the stale woodland floor.

Beneath the Sky

Threading my path through the thick fog, laying as smoke,
in the fertile moans of the cluttered woods,
I roamed until the trail grew slim and I became lost.

The leaves rest upon me as a crown.
Silently, I quivered to the sulking bloom
of fresh Autumn breath.

Shivering rings of the moon
wrapped through the mist of the heavy trees
which stood as a sentinel.

By years end, I coiled through the moist earth.
I slept as an offering to the cotton
stretch of the lowering clouds.

Soil and moss layered upon my cool flesh as the blushing
sky opened and rinsed me in wild rains.

Losing Her in the Mist

Into the dredge of the wild flower,
each rose and pampered the calves and feet
as she dipped through the moist, silky grasses.

As the buds of every shrub and bush
popped pollens into the air, they burst, floated
as incense.

I paused upon the crisp clinging air
and felt the pat of the rains
which softened every step.

I touched the tumble of each snip of misty nightfall.
Into the depth of this night, I lost her in the dancing wind.

Morning Awaits

The creek, pushed by the spring, shoved forth from these mountainous rocks,
perched high on top of the chiseled earth
sliced quick and gushed down the thread of the lush overgrowth.

I wade thigh deep in this crisp spread of cool sauce.

Travelling home, I lost my way as the slick, fertile valley swabbed across me.

Gingerly, I could feel the bush, shrub,
and flower patch gripped
with sweet fragrance much as the sting of the pollens
fell against the updraft of the floating breeze.

From the distance of the peak,
I watched the roaming clouds swallow
from tip to the shout, wallowing cliffs.

I took a heavy drink and waited quiet
until the shadow of nightfall.

By morning, the sky grew clear and I continued forth.

Incense in the Chapel

This heavy shadow bloomed as a cloak,
whispering with the drifting
breath of your twitching, tumbling lips.

I burrow my face in your lavish silk hair.
Fragrance lifts as incense from the dormancy of this chapel
which hosts the rain, wind, and softest earth.

With the fracture of a moment,
I lift the flood as you burn your cool fingers
through the shirt, pants, and softness of my flesh.

As I look beyond the cedars of the woods,
I touch you on the paint of your lips.

To the distance you walk.
Treading along the sunken clouds which
clean you from this slate.

I feel your absence in the sulking winds of breath
and fullness of your lungs.

Dreaming of Crows

I caress your tender feet
on the soft stroke of a pebbled bed,
supporting the fluid stream.

Sweetly, I watch as you loosen your wet, pasted clothes.

Your breasts gleam along the dance
of the pollens, threading through the nearest breeze,
glinting with the passing splash of this tender sun.

In a taut pinch of the splashing channel and bed,
water beads trim their way along your stiff abdomen.

~

Along the coursing field where I walk,
I filled my mouth with your scents.

Peppering the ash gray sky, I
look upon the heavy murder of worn, tired crows
surfacing from the distant wheat,
then nestling quiet in the hard gray earth.

I walk from field to field and covet your scent across the crest
of my face and seizing hands.

Now nightfall, the crows calm in the distant woods.

Night's Shadow at the Shore

You watched as I curled upon your breasts;
I spoke with the foams of the open sea.

Film covered shells drew along the shore
as each one took countless years to find residence.

We sulked beneath the flickering moon
which spread pale blue light in the flash of a crescent
bloom.

I touched the canyons of your back.
Softly, we awoke to the riddling sway of nights shadow,
pulsing strokes and wrapping kelp,
I seized the soft limp, grip of your hand.

I fed upon you until the spread of mornings dance.

Funeral March at Twilight

I walk upon you as you tug my ankle and foot.
Speaking to me, you breath the softest words
as they fall from the slicing gash of heavens pale light,
a wrestle in twilight.

Pausing upon the moisture of our fields,
the slap of starving rows of barley,
I touch the smallest drop of dew
which sets still upon your lips.

Into this rolling mask of earth and rock,
I surrender to the press of your tongue
and all it's heavy verbs,
whimpering along the drafty breath of wind.

Undressing beneath the Moonlight

Splashing through the wind,
gnarled branches and leaves which undress
as you would undress by the glaze of the dim moonlit sky,
the oak removed it's gown and hugged tight
to the lavish, scarlet touch of midnights breath.

I lay upon these yellow and tans.
The crimp of each leaf fluttered along my shoulders
and bathed me in dust.

Each hour threshed along the shift of the crescent moon.
as the softest pinks and shrouding purples
rose across the thin blade of the horizon,
I placed each stitch and fumbled my way home.

Trail Leading Home

Her touch, iced and smooth with each droplet of rain,
slivered me in threads as the thick humid breath
of her quivering mouth sulked across me.

Into the fields which stretch across her back,
chiseled shoulders and the fullness of her walnut colored hair
groomed the touch of my feet and patterned

Along the brim of my ankle and heel.

I walked to the end of each graze, barley and wheat.
The lowering skies shrouded you
with the thinnest cottons, stretching upon the starving tuft.

I turned from you and walked the trail which led me home.

Finding the Forest Deep

I relish in the strokes of the creek and the dance
of the onion sprouts resting by waters edge.

I tempt my mouth to the water, then drink.

Each of the maples were tugged upon
with the flickering breath
of the thickest hour of night.

Walking home, pebbles snapping beneath my boots,
I fed my moist hair to the caress of the pollens
which fastened to every clip of the evening's breeze.

Reaching the climb of the path, I stepped
upon the fragile moss and entered the
shadow of the forests spread

Dreams from the Earth

This delicate hand groomed the soft flesh of your nakedness.
Robe of silk fell to the sleek, sinewy muscles
of your calves and rested upon you.

Eagerly, I absorb you with the sting of my eyes
as the garments you wore tugged the soil
in all it's gathering rain.

By morning, I fell upon the earth and smelled
each bloomed fragrance as I plucked a mint
leaf from the tender garden.

Every stroke of the spreading mosses,
I slept upon this jade and emerald bedding.

The minerals of the earth slouched through me
as the press of the tapping rain blossomed across every
angle and warmth of this plunging mist.

I free myself to this grotto and glen
where we once walked and tugged each other with our eyes.

In the end, I slouched to the glimpse of your pale, full
breasts which smooth this path to the mineral wealth of soil.

Birch wood

Trembling beads of a fine dew
rests upon the yawning birch wood
which shook to the clever sun,
rattling branches.

I spoke in verbs, whispers of the sauced leaves.
The sky peppered in a misty haze.

Soils spoke, "I am refined as the host
of this gluttonous wood.
step upon me and you will find the swipe
of the most majestic wind."

Into the mumbling clouds which sank upon
the moist and humid earth, I slept until the fog rose
from cliff to rambling peak.

A year and perhaps a half later, the quiet
Birch wood sank each branch in the solitude
of the stale, warm breath of air.

As the Orchard Fades

The pulps swelled within the red, tanned flesh of the apple,
each apple as they hung in pronunciation
of their delicate stem.

Between my teeth, resting upon my tongue and jaw,
I snapped the skin.

Moments past, I stand in the fat of the rain.

I walk from this orchard and sleep beneath
the curling branches and leaves
of this towering tree, alone by the slapping creek.

When I awake, the fog lifts and spreads to the thi, crisp air.

Thickest Hour

I came to you as a fawn stepping through the woods.
Looking from treetop to ferns waving
and moss gnawing upon
the tree roots and rocky floor,
I answer to the sultry voice you swim through
as ash across the campfire of deep night.

Arriving with my palms upon the powders of your
fruitful breasts, wind tackles through my fine hair.

You come to me as a stitch upon a fiber.
I relish in the beauty of your nude proclamations.
I pause, then continue to soothe across your
clavicle and the posture of your sweet neckline.

Into the thickest hour of night, I unleash this tender taste,
the moisture rising with the wind.

Recollection by the River

The river sliced across the jagged rocks;
white capped ripples traveled in retort
as the swollen sun drifted to the channel and softened bed.

With kelp tangling across my feet,
I soothed my way from edge to edge,
here, the moisture trembled to my torso and face

As the wind pursued me in tug and throbbing pull.

~

I loosened the edge, brim of my mouth.

Sullenly, I recall the taste of her trembling mouth
as we would watch these gushing waves
pamper the drip from waist to chill of our ankles.

~

I look to the blush of the sky and fade
softly into your surrendering voice.

So slowly, you fade among the dripping clouds.

Flickering Moonlight

I reach to the purr of the mumbling creek.
Wrapped along the bedded stones,
my fingers web through the wavering kelp.

I wash each edge of my sweaty, burning face.

Moments later, I walk to the shadows of the forest.
Brisk, cool wind sulk through cloth and wiry beard.

I spend the evening by a settled pond.
Sleep crawls upon me as the flickering moonlight
dashes through the tree limbs.

Moans in the Field of Mist

Across the blades with gleaming dew,
each spear, slippery in all it's pronunciation,
showers each mineral and speck of soil,
as jade hums beneath the tumbling, skies heavy mist.

From each slice and cut of the field of grass,
I walk to you as you fade among the flickering mist,
brought from the ash gray cloaked measure
of the sulking clouds which breath upon me.

Listening to the rattling treetops, I pause,
quietly, I stand still, close to the earth
and fill my lungs with humid groans of this pasture.

I rise from a kneeling bend and sink to the thick
of this moaning breath.

Upon the fattening choke of sinking clouds,
I roam the meadow until a fracture of daylight
blooms upon me. I sit upon this broken log
and watch as dust hazes the silks and satin robe
of morning.

Nocturne in the Woods

Along the drowsy slumber of the soft rolling creek,
I snatched the driftwood in my palm.

Crisp, muttering air slipped across me.
Drawing circles in the soft mud, I
glanced to the nearest front
of the nearest opening of the nearest forest,
trimmed in evergreens and housing the fallen chipped nuts.

In the slouching cloak of dusk,
I enter these abandoned woods.

Softly, I leave this staff, soaked in the calmest waters.
I absorb my way with scents from the dripping sap
and probe the deep of each boastful nocturne.

Across the Tumbling Ocean

The sunset tossed pinks upon navies
through the thin lipped approach of nightfall.

Autumn's chilled winds skirted across my neck and chest.
I rest on this pebbled yard as the skies

Open in a gash as the trembling foam
slithers along the ocean sand.

~

Her voice spoke it's way across the tumbling ocean.
I fed my way through to her as the sea birds swipe
and gather fish, leaving only a soft ripple of absence.

~

Evening hushed in the shroud of night.
I slept until the pasture of moist waters
claimed me in abundance.

Surrender to the Woods

The dance of the blackbird darted across the sight
of the red maple to the pineneedle bed.

Beyond, I witnessed the dark purple stare of the canvased
skyline. Each shout of the distant winds

fell to the loosened threads of my hair.

I swelled in this blanket of night.
I listened to the pitch of each bird as sauntering winds
bloomed through me in rivets of the swelling moon.

I fastened to the leaves which surrounded me.
with each pull of darkness, I slept upon each
lathering dew drop and each sap of wood.

~

With the flicker of the tuft where leaves
summon the earliest sun glance, I tucked
deeper into the madness
of the forest and all its shadow.

Rest by the Fade of Maples

In a decisive moment, I wrangled beneath the cluttered,
spread of birchwood trees which shed a thread of bark
only to lay, sleep upon the soil, spread like a blanket.

I loosened my shirt as the breath of Autumn wrapped against
me in the quiet return to the earth, alive in trembling wind.

Crave into this hymnal of dying breath and tumbling
clutter where every leaf slept upon each leaf, I moistened
to a tumbling crouch of orange, brown, and creamed yellow.

With the fade of this vision, crumbling
to the dust where I rest,
I watched faintly as the maples rattled each with branch
upon branch and slowly drifted to a quiet sleep.

Trail of the Sun

I wait for you in the rumbling bloom of the meadow.
I hear the ginger steps of your delicate foot and heel.

As the clouds descend, I come to you in the sulking mist of
Every trembling patch of grass.

From the slouch of my shoulders,
I hear the whispers of your tender breath.

Further, I reach the deep of the murmuring field
Where you slither your way into the depth of my lungs.

I grab your aromas and spices which sting their way
Across my tender flesh.

Reaching down into the caked crust of the earth,
I whisper verbs of solitude, verbs of departure.

Turning to the east, I follow the trail of the sun.

Return to the Soil where I Sleep

Green blossoms, emerald to a quiet
jade, snap between the snip
of my finger and tip of my thumb.

In a moment, I listen to the thuds, tree clashing with tree.

Wind swabs the red chill of my face as I soothe
upon the approaching cloud, falling from
the nearest mountain jaunt.

While I hunger for the paste of the
earth, touch of the sulking
stream, slice of each blade of grass,

I breath thick breadth of the Spring water beads.
A moment passes and I drift to the land I bloom upon,
stroke the fumbling tossed soil where I sleep so quiet.

Evening Walk

I look upon the oak tree, crackling with each heavy branch. The acorn snaps beneath me.

I place one in the deep pocket I share with my cool hands.

As I return to the sidewalk, I watch the tumbling leaves croon, caress along the silent asphalt.

I mourn as the rain falls upon me.

Waiting for Boats

I stand upon the mouth of the lake.
Behind me, the threads of the purring
stream burrow in a flash
as dancing, trembling sunlight tears through the gentle
cove, crowded with trees.

I rest upon the smoothest of stones.
Each current breaths upon the gathering wind.

I turn my face and moan for the stretch of the other coast.

As a boat slice through the tender, cool water
I trace my fingers through the foams and films.

Storm Spreads

I spread my way across the pale blue linens.
Dancing rain tapped along the cracked, weathered windows.
The mumbling voice of the blackest cloud
spoke of indifference.

Laying against your pillowy breasts,
the slumber of heavy night dreamed upon us.

Awake, now morning, I wake alone with the shout
of the battered grass and mimic of each bird
which rallies through to the trickling slick water
slipping across each emerald blade.

The house moans as the ancient bones beneath my flesh
cry in a mourning residue from the pulsing
storm.

I swallow as blades upon my throat
provide me with a distant groan, slash
in an open meadow, too far to touch.

Vapors Fade

As I fade, vapors lull upon the crunch of the misty earth,
these wilting flowers, shrubs, and crimping grasses
boast of my faith and groom gently upon my sour flesh.

I dwindle from the sharp, snap of daylight.
I feel the caress of each sprout which soothes the back
of my waist and softening neck.

I grip one last look upon the evergreen woods.
I hear the crows at bedtime.
I taste the sweet blooming air as the lids of my eyes

fade to dust.

Host at Close of Day

The trees arched as to host a gateway
to another place entirely.
Paused, i traced my fingers and thumb
along this ancient bark;
resting as a map, these grooves spoke of the riddle of time.

Looking up, the vines wove through and wove across
every branch and every twig.

Now Autumn, the leaves peppered the ground.
I cover with them and sleep forward only to grasp
the flicker of this moonlight.

Into the satchel of this breathing sky, I
thought of the dancing fields.
Frost nips the blades as I drift among
the dusts which cover me.

Winter's Sulk

Frost flecked across the garden grotto and crunched
beneath the chisel of my boots.

I absorb the chill blooming across my
face, red and endless sting.
This birchwood thrashed along the winded breath
which tugged by root in the frozen earth.

Skies succumb to an ash gray hue as the distant
chilled breeze tore through the naked meadow,
tore through each sauntering, white capped stream.

Upon finding the path which led me to the trail
tugging through to the shelter of this dense forest,
I smiled and made my way.

Lost

I wade through the forest, trembling
ferns cover from edge to edge.
A breath of cool air, a pocket void of
humid lashings, fondles my
face and flickering hair.

Now, crouching by the sweet, gushing
spring, each pebble and rock
moistens in a thorough touch.

I wander north, south, west, and east as the saps of every tree
deepens to the soil beneath each step.

Although I am lost, I continue forth
with winded currents upon me.
Each stroke digs beneath my cotton fabrics.

So happily, I have lost my way.

Pampering Earth

Curling winds wrapped, tugged upon
the threads of my fine, limp hair.
I open my eyes to the gray passing clouds.
Into the drench of the mosses beneath my feet,
I rest and sulk by the cover of the pinetree.

You passed my way as the rains soften in the threaded grass.
I ask you to touch my arm as I relish in the paste
which glistens upon each inch of skin and flesh.

Now as I lose my way into the pampering earth,
I soften into a sweet passing breeze of mint.
Answers from the moisture, pinning the soft bed of soil,
I return to you in the fire of the sun.

Searching through the Forest Depth

The crackling trees rose and sauntered in the depth
of these woods.

Thin sliver of the moon dripped upon
the floor with flickering
silvers, from fern to stroking mosses.

I rest by the slithering creek.
I sink my fingers and thumb as the driftwood whispers past.

From the paste of the rains, meshed
with mulch and heavy soil,
I glance, looking for you.

Treasure

I touch you, the treasures soothed beneath the linens,
groomed and pressed in silks.

I lay upon the powders, dredged in the breasts
which fill as milks within the pouches soft.

I caress the cove of your trembling thighs.
You open to me as a pasture.

You soothe as barley upon the moist richest field.
I deepen upon you.

By twilight, I open to you as a prism.
I recall the glimpse of your heavy chestnut eyes.

Cottons Fall

The vines wrapped tightly around each pronouncement
of each branch and limb.

Leaves of the red maple scurried along
the pressure of the tender earth.

I gasp as the winds thread through the heavy mist,
roaming from hair to tuft of grass upon the ground.

Through these woods, I hear your moaning voice
as the clever stream batters along the rocks and dam.

I follow you with the dancing light, fading in the stitches
of night's slumber.

The skies dampen and sink with the seduction of these
coiled, trembling treetops.

I slip my way through the fog, lay on this gown.
The softest earth, I watch as the cottons
slip across bark and fern.

Ocean Cove

I trace the palms of my hands across the pale valley
which curves to the posture of your shivering abdomen.

Sweetly, my cheeks rest upon your heavy breasts.
Looking out the naked window,

I watch the trees stretch along the rolling hills.
I open my mouth to the misty rain.

I raise my trembling hands as the fullness of your lips
soothe from bank to channel and bed.

Listening, the oak, outside the garden gate,
shudders with the quake of your calves and thighs.

As the rise of this river strolls to the mouth
of the ocean cove,

I wither inside of your warmth.

Winter Sets

Stones scurried, peppered across the pale gray skyline.
each spoke in a muffled cry as they flapped through the wind.
Swift, they land upon the wilting grass,

I turned and walked my path,
tenderly through the crimping field.

I watched as this murder gathered and
strode through the chilled current.

With the hush of a quiet press
where snows flecked upon the frozen earth,
I listened to the "caws" grow distant
upon the stroking breeze.

In retort, I felt the stones and patch of
green crunch beneath my feet.

Summer Glaze

With the slouching heat of the thick glaze of Summer,
I feel the pulse of approaching night.

I wander across the overgrowth of each greens and browns
of each lofting meadow.

Damp clouds, alive in the meandering humid air,
I walk my way treading toward you with
my feet upon the quivering
crowded slab of grass.

Upon the wind, I embrace the touch of your breath,
slouching to the crest of my neck and shoulders.

I peer to the sky.
I witness your flickering mouth and
walk swiftly toward the touch
of meadow upon meadow.

Searching in the Woodlands

Delicate, the elm leaves swooned upon the moist soil;
I wade thigh deep across this woodland palate.

I recall a canvas of your touch and
bouquet of your spices and scents.
You come to me in paleness and powdery glimpses
of each spread of flesh, each trembling crescent lip.

Looking back, the leaves have scattered in tans and browns.
I smell the grooming floods of the tree
and all it's withering parchment.

With pulsing rhythms, I open my neck to the slapping wind.
Traveling to the silks of the earth, rains
upon a soothing woodland carpet,
I remove a branch from the earth and continue forward.

With the wind and tapping rain against my back,
I walk upon both tremor and thrust of her stint of breath.

Soak

I roam the map upon your chest, abdomen, and thighs.
In the drift of this room, you raise your scent as incense
which coats the spread of my bust and sulking lips.

Threads slip their way across you as the peak
soaring upon each summit draws you to shape and definition.

I lull my face and cheek to the softness of your breasts.

The coil of your threaded hair curves
upon both shoulders and nape.

I thicken my feet and calves through the toss of both garment
and the pause of your sulking robe.

I recall the looseness of your unfastened hair
which caressed both edge and curve.

In the sadness of the fading hour, the gathering of our glaze
soaks between us.

Rain Pastes upon the Field

The mist settled with the sauce of a sweet drizzling rain
which left soft imprints upon the grass and clover.

My naked feet dug calmly as the shoots and sprouts
fastened around my calves and thighs.

Quietly, I recall the touch of your palm and fingers,
soothing the arch of my yearning feet.

I glimpsed upon the darkening clouds
which soothed an upheaval
of placid rain.

Walking home through the fields, I dipped my way,
opened to the stamp of the prior.

Tending to her step and gate, I follow this trail
as the skies unfolded and pasted upon me.

Light begins to Fade

The sky weighs upon me as I thrash my path into the deep
of the endless prairie, full with thickets bloomed.

I hear the earth crackle as I lean forth.
Wheats and barleys shade me to the depth of my thighs.

The lone oak tree stands proud as testament of antiquity.
Slight shade soothes as I rest for an hour.

Almost nightfall, the sting of the sun begins to fade
and I wrap myself in this cloak of passing clouds

Which sulk and croon, wrapping cotton
coils across the crescent moon.

I stand, then walk into the tremors of a swift night.
The breath of this place softens passage into my eager lungs.

At the Pond

I look upon the stale, cool water.
With stillness spread, I watch the dance of her face
peer back and smile upon me with this haze of night.

I remove this cloth and stitch as the moonlight bathes
me in clever pale light and touches it's way with softness.

She entices me from the spreading
moss and the moaning winds
which answer my request as a calm retort.

In the scurry of a slight movement, I
reach for her and dampen
my arms and fist.

I sulk my skin into the silent kelp.
I turn so slowly and gather a few things, I leave this place
as the stint of night dampens and shudders.

Pine Tree Forest and the Spring Water

The river slapped and gushed it's way
through the pine wood forest.
Kneeling in patience, I drank by the mouthful,
stood, and set about my way as a deer
through each thicket and bush.

The glaze of the midday sun welted burns across my neck
as I sweetly discovered the mints which
spread the woodland floor.

I reached the peak of the crest of these wooded hills.
Calmly, I lay upon the needled bed
and slumbered until the brisk
shadow of night swept quietly upon me.

The evening roamed along my flesh as a cloak
drifted across each trembling shadow.

The saps of the trees shouted their scents with the icy spring
opening it's thighs.

Sweetwater trembled it's way through
the cluttered forest of pine trees.
I followed the flickering waters until the ache of darkness
madly fell upon me.

The Days After

I wilted my slick, soothing tongue upon the trembling pearls
of her chest. I embraced the warm, humid breath
which fluttered across your lips. I seized the chiseled map
of her shoulders and back as the dim light shadowed it's way.

A few days past, I walked through her garden and filled
myself with each scent and sultry spice.

Wildflowers around the gardens edge,
I dipped my feet through hyacinths and tiger lilies.

I looked above and saw the flickering humid breath
cloud and shade the reach of the bay window.

I turned my face to the rising sun and walked into this gasp
of the opening day.

Permeate

The sweetness of your breath roamed through every octave
And hung in the fashion of permanence.

I absorbed you through your silky touch
Which flooded my chest in tight warm butters.

I glanced to you and all the fullness of your goblets
Which were warm and filled with milks.

Clothing fell as leaves to a forest floor in the swoon of spring.

I open myself to all the nakedness of your crave and posture.
The wildflowers of your fumbling scents soothed upon me.

I climb the endless snip of wheat which
fills your thighs and cavern.
With the gesture of a moment, the
sweet winds pass by, overhead.

Sweet Pastures

Upon the threshold of evening shadow
and the fracture of daylight
slapping to the thin lips of the horizon,
I stood and walked a frequent mile to the glen which holds
emeralds and jade in the spreading grasses.

I touch upon the breath of her,
the twilight winds croon and caress across my tender face.

I gather the scents which prowl through the field.
I soak myself upon you as the heavy pouches of your
breasts throw sweet spices through the air.

I wade in the depth of the bending shoots, and sprouts.

I pass through the thicket which scurries along the edge.
I hunger for the dew of early morning,
the tremble of sweet pastures soak the threads of my denim.

Swift Creek

Green buds, the flowered pod opens in a dash.
I deepen my way through the ripe meadow which soothes
each stretch and flutter of sweet pods.

I strengthen to the grip of each warm Summer breeze
as each Summer collides upon the Autumn dance,
tucked in yellows and crinkling browns.

Upon leaving this place, I cast to the thick spread
of the cool dashing shadows where this woodland
roams from edge to edge and curve to curve.

I bleed with the thornbush as it strokes
and slices across the thinnest path.
I recover along the soft caress of the flickering fern. I pause
swift by the tugging creek and drink heavily.

Well into August the forest thickened
and drew upon heavy pronunciation
where the wind rattles the treetop; the gems of gnarled earth
sliced and threw endless rocks upon the path and eager trail.

Late Summer

Oak trees lining the brown and pale yellow leaves,
tumbling across this calm pebbled road,
I listen to the snap of my boot upon heavy gravel.

Each loose leaf scrapes along the cracked patterned asphalt
which hosts the tender juices of morning dew.

I sit beneath the oak, the greatest of all oaks.
As eaves to an ancient house, branches drip a saunter
of the coolest water. I stand and continue forth.

I feel the moist winds reach the flank of my face and torso.
Quietly, I bathe here, soaked shirt, soaked denim.

Into the strike of nightfall, I gather myself
and venture to the driest earth which speaks of late Summer.

Once

Into the posture of this ancient forest,
Blooming buds flicker as light dancing through every branch,
Opened as a prism.

I walk further. I gather these muds and
dip my boots upon them.

Sliding around the thornbush, I continue to open my legs
Wildly to the courting stream.

I wade through to the edge of my stitch and thighs.
I reach the foams of each set of throbbing ripple and gush.

Absorbing the pulses of the heated sky,
I thought of you as you once lay.

Fang

Drenched in the crimping burn of the sun,
She sweetly spoke of her nakedness.

Filled and wrapped in the water and kelp of the soothing
Pond, she touched upon this glaze of want.

Dripping in rivulets of moist clinging threads,
Her tongue grooved as a fang and deepened upon me.

Wind crafted her in cool a shuddering bloom.
I stood beside her; I sculpted her until
the moans of nightfall caressed.

Far East

I opened the earth and found minerals and sacred rocks.
I stood upon this marble and filled my lungs
with the bloomed gasping winds which breathed across
the forested mountain far to the east.

The wind which uprooted in the high standing peaks
burrowed through the dance of my hair.

Below each slab of ice, the tender evergreens trembled in saps
as the moss froze and the branches moaned of antiquity.

I stood for a long moment, sulking in
the press of hours upon hours.
Wrestling with the breath, alive this wrapping sky,

I turned my face and softly stepped from
rock to the approaching meadow.
Jade of these grasses flickered from toe to ankle and calf.

From Drought to the Fallen Rains

From the bloods of the skies,
pulsed from the drip upon the horizon,
I thickened, deepened my sight to the flickering haze.

Warmth blushed across my eager face
as the tepid wind slanted over me;
I listened to the mourning dove "cooing" closer,
closer again.

My mouth lay as a palate for pollens to dip.
My lungs gripped the spices of the late Summer breath;
the rigid peak of the northern mountains
lashed and bloomed across the open field
where I rested.

I recall the wilt and mourn of the starving trees.
With the heaviest crimp from the driest leaves
I spoke to these pine trees and their endless thirst
roamed through the valley and the clay covered earth.

Upon my return, groans of the moisture
slithering to root and branch. I grasped the glaze
of this late Summer posture, fluttering to the tree tops,
caking to the gentle muds.

Fade

The maple tree removed her robes,
each leaf peeled back for a layer of bark, wooden flesh.

Casting my sight upon the fading reds,
I spoke of fantasies to every quivering branch

as the silk wind breathed along the forested gown;
I listened to the sweetest of her scents.

Whipping air slapped heavy against me.
Feeling my jacket press against my back and shoulders,

I thought of her and swiftly faded to the dust of the earth.

Deep of Autumn

I walk among the tumbling leaves which
gather under my boots only to crinkle as the loosened
grip upon a parchment sheet.

I think of you as your delicate pieces of cloth
and silk peel, pat upon the ground, left
to wrap along the woodland tree, bush, and shrub.

Heat from your breath and
silence of this humid sulk of pressing vapors
wrap across my cheek and cool neck.

You stand naked as the deep Autumn tree.
You take me on this journey and discard your powders
which loft from your quivering breasts
to the edge of my mouth.

Alone in this forest,
I hear the moans of the clattering tree.

Horizon

Beneath the pulse of the pounding sun which
webbed quiet arms across our naked flesh,
I spoke of the coming bloods along the horizon
which dredge in pinks and reds.

I recall the slippery touch of your wrestling arms.
You moaned a gasp which throated from the heavy meadow.
The smacking wind gathered our hair,
yellow and heavy chestnut.

Looking to the sky, I watched the
gauze of the thinnest clouds
drift away as the cloth and stitch you loosened.

Stones and Mud

Through the open gate, I feel my ankles and shoes sponge
across the slippery grass.

I look upon the stones thrown across the yard.

In a moment, the quivering rain slaps
each patch of tender mud.

Swiftly, I can hear the moans of my ancestors
as they speak across the blushing wind.

Tapping Rains

The silks across your pale warm thighs
gathered to the chill of the hardwood floor.

Against the press of your breasts, open
in all their nakedness, I lay the swoon of my weary head
and breath against your trembling flesh.

I place my hand to the edge of your moist lips;
outside, I listen to the tapping rains.

Visitation

I thread my way through the garden,
cluttered in shades of jade and soft, the color of emeralds.

Small pouches of spice sweep across my cheeks, neck, and lay
upon my sweetened lips.

I pause by the nearby slicing creek.
Gently, I recall her as she would wade waist deep
and return to me in slithering beads, glazed as a pearl.

I still smell the sweet scents they crowd through
the breath of this soft, crooning air.

~

Into the moisture of this cultivating earth,
I swiftly dip my hands and recall her touch,

much as the drift of a single oak leaf patterns
along the current of each stroke

where the creek waters strive for endless continuity.

She Comes from the Northern Mountain

Her flesh spread as a meadow which enticed and bloomed
the perfect scents.

Her bones shook and moaned as a prison,
trembling and still as the rocky bedding
which hosted grasses and the softest moss.

Walking across the thicket of thornbush and reach
of the bamboo shoot,
I wrestled and gathered the slippery haze
of the breeze which danced from tuft of hair
to tuft of flickering hair.

You came to me in the thickest hour of nightfall.

The crest of your laughter surfaced across
the highest peak of the northern mountain.

I unwrapped the garments as I waited for you
and the glisten of your touch.

Mountain Trail

I crossed the threshold. I fled to the mountains.
Boulders pronounced themselves on top of boulders.
The spread of the moss spoke of solitude.

Softly, I rest next to the purring stream, gushing spring.
The sky opened into pinks and purples,
I gaze upon a tender voice, the sky swiftly turned to darkness.

Scents of honey thread their way as my mouth
opens to the sweet, coiling winds.

I rest by the thin, slender roaming trail.
By morning, I can see the endless valley open before me.

Threads of the opening eyes of morning,
I pause, I seek the pinnacle, highest peak.

House upon the Hill

Visions of the home resting upon the peak,
heavily slouched and pronounced upon this hill,
I listened gingerly and walked the crest of this path.

Sweetly, I heard the verbs quake upon the font of my ears.
The spread of this tender forest swooned to my senses,
sight, taste.

Pausing to the rolling creek, I knelt
and found my way across sauces of patterned water.

With the pulses of the broad opening sky,
I quake to the gentle opening door.

Tenderly, I walk through the gentle door and look.
I felt the rock, door, and speech of the walls.

I sit and softly rest my feet upon the cool slabs of stone.

Open Gate

I open the gate and enter this shrouding place
where rest abounds and darkness in the thick of night
roams across as a cloak.

I hear the slices of a soft wind
thread it's way across the burn of my neck and face
as this Summer glances across my groaning throat.

As I rest upon a stone,
I listen to the moans of my ancestor,
I soften to the threads of this roaming winds.

I leave this place with a mold of gentle breeze.

Fumbling Weeds

Into the fracture of the sky, thinning with clouds of gauze,
I step to the road.

Lilacs and holly bushes climbed their way across the slicing
path, rendered in yellows and greens;

I pass through the fumble of each weed;
I speak to the approaching rains which chill

The warm Summer air which clouds across in the thick
of a humid splash.

I hear the bones of the earth as they crackle beneath me.

The thinning air breeds in a swarm,
I feel the specks of rain as the quivering trees eagerly
reach for a moist touch.

Swooning Verbs

I opened myself to the bold nakedness of her breast.
The sky lowered and dipped its windy fangs through my hair.
Tucking my cheek along the edge of her soft, tender jaw,
I glazed upon a distance which held my swooning verbs
in a pocket for her gentle ears and tongue,
filled with tastes of promise.

I lather upon the warm breath of her soothing mouth.
Gasping my burrowing hands through the gaze of each smile
and frolic.

Lastly, her warm, soft flesh grew tepid
upon my wilting mouth.
My eyes peered through her into the distance of every stitch
which held me quiet and close.

Lost into the Forest

I breath the pollens and bursting pods.
Swelling lungs in the deep of this woodland grove,
I open my mouth to an endless cavern.

I proclaim the gentle moss and flickering ferns
as the declarative of soothing friendship.

Lull of the spreading pond,
I lay so tenderly by the wayside.

Promise of this roaming spread of pines
grip me with each scent of splashing green.

Wandering through the thicket and proud soothing
forest, winds chyme through and cross my eager face.

From nightfall, to daylight and nightfall again,
I open myself to the hunger of this heavy moss.

The shades of fluttering light,
breaking through the branches and
crouching steams of morning,

I walk into this fractured prism.

Adjacent to the Dash of the River

I tear through the lull of the slow, soothing river.
Muds soften across the bridge of my feet;
clever winds tremble along the sweetness of my lips,
dripping in moist breath from the sky,
I angle to the lips of mist which dash
across my chest and neck.

I look upon the swerving croon of the
veins here in this scattered forest.
Pulsing my way to the channels and rapids;
I taste the milks of the earth.

Through the fiber and threads of the
woodland trees, thrown adjacent,
I rest by bark and pillowed moss, in a moment
the gloat of the moon drips upon me.

Tamp of the Earth

A patch of the onion grass roamed through
the thicket and thornbush.
I glanced upon the sweet tang of mint,
eagerly, I taste upon my tongue.

Grottos of grassy mounds toured the hosting meadow.
Now dark, I kneel upon the quaking earth;
blue lightning, I grasp the flickering branches.

Quietly, I pave my way through this field, sulking pastures.
I open to the thin air which seeks its way through
throat and lungs.

The nudity of the tamp of the earth,
I think of you and sweetly walk into the distance of nightfall.

Fumbling Dust and Her Fading Flesh

Her robe fell upon the earth,
opening with the fumble of pale yellow leaves.

I shook across her in the drip of morning,
I felt the freeze of night soften to moisture and touch
where the maple trees murmur in nakedness.

~

The sunlight flickered and pulled as a magnet.
In dissipation, her flesh faded to the dusts
grooming along the trembling forest.

Upon the scarcity of her with the bloom of day
sweeping across me, she glanced and smiled
with the passing winds.

~

Most tender, I walked along the treeline.
Softness of her settled in the dancing forest.

This forest spread as incense.
I smelled her and the croon of her soothing flesh.

Fangs of Winter

The rain drew courtship with patterns of the moistest bead.
From these waters, I smelled and soothed along the springs
gushing from the peak of the northern mountain.

I temp my wet, pasted hair
which flickered from the grasping winds.

I smell the mulch, dancing swoon, climbing each source
of my mouth and nostril, I breath the glaze of the ices,
roaming across the mountain air.

As the breathing voice of air roams through with a chill,
she speaks to me in rhythms.

The fangs of Winter deepen into me,
I breath and breath again.

Oak Staff

Jousting winds tore fiber and threads
of the limp tufts my hair.

I leaned against an oak, rattling as a staff.

Muds of the earth groomed the ache of heel and ankle;
I dipped through the pull of the stream,
here I stood.

Into the quake of my abdomen, I opened my mouth
and sweetly found rain tapping upon my face.

I gathered a fist of leaves.

Into the Summer jaws of temptation, I slept
upon this grouping of parchment
tender mounds of oak.

Tomb from the North

I wrestled against the slap and purr of the icy
mountain creek.

Winded branches thrashed and shed their delicate
leaves upon the trembling path which
rose along the earth;
I moaned to the sky as a fugue cascaded
to the Autumn valley.

Quietly I left the mask of a sulking Fall.

In the crisp blue of the sky,
gray clouds swelled across the edge of the horizon
to the edge of the horizon.

I chiseled my way to the meadow filled with endless pollens
and breathed the endless roaming winds which succumbed
to this place of solitude and coiling
mathematics stroking every shoot
and thicket.

Into the robes of nightfall, I surrendered
and lay upon the climbing boulders.
With Winter's grip, I sat bequeathed to the fangs of ice.
Silently, I left, stroked upon by the
howling tomb so far to the north.

Rejoice

In the deep of night, the rains fell as tapestries,
sobbing cloaks upon the ground.

Softly, I lean my face to the prancing moon.
Eagerly, I drink heavily.

Winds burrow from the snapping breath of the north.
Glancing, I look to the slumbering mist,
drowsy patting fog clings in this sobbing masquerade.

Morning came and the sky soothed as a prism.
Gingerly, the moans of the forest slivered through each
sulking crown of fading flower and pulsing fern.

I cupped my hands upon the brim of my face.
I fell to the earth and humbly rejoiced.

Requiem

Sauntering, my fingers stroked, soothed across the chill
of the dampest leaves.

As they swept through to the fullness and gathering
shroud, my thoughts shook upon the distant
paints of her moist mouth.

Now, looking to the clamoring branches,
high upon the treetops,
each struggling leaf fell.

Your scent flooded across me as the dusts of silence
swept you so far away.

I walked my way as powders wrapped about me.
The scent of your flesh fumbled through
each branch and twig.

In the clinging gauze of this heavy fog,
I loosened and fell to the dance of each wrestling tree.

Lost in the Beams of Morning Light

I touched with her bones so delicate and carved of glass.

Upon the wooden floor, I soothed across the garments
soaking the fresh touch of satin and lace.

Her breasts, powdered and filled pouches,
I fell to the dance of fragrance.

Upon breathing the aromas and spices of her flesh,
roaming as the wheat fields touching
the threads of taste and feel,
I walked into the deep valley of her
thighs and quaking abdomen.

Into the glance of morning light dancing
upon the walls and linens
scattered about the bed, I left for the touch of morning sun.

I listened to her moans as I quickly lost my way.

Woods

Trembling from kelp to film,
I traced rippling lines across the heavy green water.

Scents of leaves, acorns and chipped pine cones
dashed along the silence of the thick woods.

I walked my way to the slow pouring river.
I looked to the sky which opened as a gash.

With the shattered dance of light,
the prism unfolded and shouted in thickening rains.

I pressed my hands to the bedded moss;
traces of you soothed the edges of my hands.

Pulses at Morning

Her lashes groomed both scent and glaze.
I opened the window and sank to the
bloom of the scattered breath,
the hush of crooning night.

From the faint glimmer and distant moan,
I listened to the bones of your ancestors.

With the marrow between your teeth,
I slowly fed upon you as the fullness of your breasts

filled my mouth with foam and milk.

By morning, I left, filled the deep of the soils with tread.
Beneath the groans of the rumbling skyline,
I walked and lay beneath the soaring
branches of the sweet maple.

I lay my soft cheek on the tender earth.
Gently, I hear your pulse throb against the drizzle
of the glimpsing rains.

I lay here for the duration of each tender heartbeat.

Rain Day

Across the boulders, a sliver, crack through the rock,
I stood and wished a coin upon the trickling trail
far in the deep of the gateway to this heavy cavern.

Walking home, I grew thickened to this pasting rain.
Tastes of this fresh cream seeped through to tongue and lips.

~

She danced upon me with the heavy moans
of her chest and the fullness of her breasts.

I pulled against her waist and soothed the press
of the softest of thighs.

My fingers moved as a bursting bead of rain.

Tenderly I Walk

I sit upon the fallen pine.
Cones and needles wrap against me as wild burlap.

I gather the dust of the bark,
sweet winds thresh through my hair.

Blooming with a distant gust,
I breath mint and cloves into the deep of my lungs.

Sauntering home,
the grasses cling to the moisture of my pant leg and boot.

Stopping by the swift racing river,
I swallow the sauces of the earth, drinking deep.

I hear her croon through the hustling sky.

Wax Pearl

I entered the flesh of the softest moss upon the softest earth.
Mist glazed across the evergreen woods;
sweetly, I thought of the sweat along
her waist, hips and thighs.

Wavering candle light shadowed across her face.

My fingers trembled along her abdomen,
the fallen leaves scampered through the
edges of the woodland floor.

Well into the thick of night, all grew silent.
Paused, then I grazed my finger along the gentle
pouches of her breasts.

Heat scampering about the room,
I felt the pearl of wax slither across my chest.

Softly, I lift my face and entered
the wash of a sweet morning mist.

From Deep in the Woods

Branches shook with the moaning wind.
I looked to the treetop and awaited the leaves
which disrobed and slowly exposed herself
as the nakedness following the gathered gown
flickering gently upon the floor.

Low clouds drifted and settled awaiting the fog
which spread in an eager gathering of cottons.

I walked into the haze and thick of morning.
From a distance, I smelled and devoured
the scent of her as I rubbed my face and fell
upon the powders of her tender flesh.
Quiet and open the woods suckled my ankle and feet.

Winter on an Autumn Day

I took a leaf from the spiked grass threading the gathering
of trees, scattered with frost.

Eagerly, I folded it until it snapped.
Dusts and veins, crimped and colored a heavy brown.

Fallen, then stepped upon by the tamp of my boot,
I faced the winds which scurried from the north.

I stopped to rest and I spoke of this;
the buckling wind of Winter slashes upon my face.
I thought of you in all your colors and hues.
I lean against this tree and await the powders of the deceased.

Dust

I answered to the prayers, moist upon your lips.
Your lungs offered hymns which slithered from
your trembling tongue.

The sweet prelude of your tongue rattled
across the mist of your breasts, dampening
with a silent sweat and roaming trail.

Grass of the garden shook to the trim of the open gate.
Dew clung to my boots and pant leg.

Softly, I heard the quake of your soothing voice.
You faded gently into the distance of a pulsing breath.

The dusts of you took to the threads of the sky.

Slumber

I showered in the shadow of night.
The sky, thickened and swelled across the chill
of my glazed flesh, I relish in a hush.

There grew a dampness to my lips and starving tongue.

I search for her as I deepened my way into the mists
of the swollen woods.

I tasted her in the rising scents from her fragrance;
I clung to the posture of her naked breasts.

Softly, I awoke and polished to the blitz of the morning sun.

Passage with the Pounding Rain

I once gripped the frailty of her wrists.
She breathed the aromas of an open meadow.

I watch as you give way to the silent earth
which trembled each spear of grass;
soft, the whisking winds,
the color of your face, bled in blue and gray.

~

A year later, I swam through the passage
of the heaviest of storms.

The bending grasses filled themselves with tender juices.

I look upon the green of your gown.
Quietly, I walked to the pebbled road.

Shame beneath the Night's Sky

The sky opened as a vocalise,
trembling through the thin, melding winds.

Sweet breath opened upon me,
I turned my face to the mask of night.

I felt her stretching arms wrap across me.
I deepened into her scarlet lips.

Sweat beads dripped across her forehead
and soothed as a crown.

Musk hung along the sulking leaf.
I found these particles of wood and roamed across her.

In the end, I fell upon a bush and
mourned through the thicket.

Fading as the gauze of the nights sky,
I shuddered through the morning smash of piercing light.

By night's eager moans, heard in the wrangle of dusk,
I held her by the pollens and saps of the shaking pines.

This cool, soothing mistress
I hold the soaking moisture of your hands,
fall to shame beneath the night's sky.

Bloods and Milks

The shadowed teardrop warmed with the heave of her breasts.
Soft upon her abdomen, flesh permeated upon flesh.
I sank to the riddles of her thighs. I spoke softly.

Her milks drizzled as a foam upon a sandy shoreline.

The smallness of her feet loosened to her dancing spine.
I held the soothed, dampness of her nave as each shuddering
tears drew stains upon her cheek.

~

Again, the crumbling shadows of her
breasts, thick with blood,
filled with milks,
I look upon her and rise with the pulsing
glitters of shrouding night.

Waltz beneath the Silver Moon

I waded through the river, the vein of the earth.
Silent and still, the blues and greens thread
the girth of my legs as the softest soil suckles my feet.

I open my mouth to the mist,
a glance of quiet falling rain.

By evening, I sleep on moss and quivering fern.

The fattened gloat of the pulsing rhythms of the silver moon,
I stride eager to the riverbank.

Swabbing tread, the forest wraps across the curving
spine of the stride of the river.

I open to the slapping grip of the passing breeze.
With the flickering dance of the falling leaves,

I breath the musk of this pulsing gasp of Autumn.

Jade

I slither across garment and gown.
Quietly, I perch to milk and foam as the warmth of her
clings to each particle of my body.

The atoms of her tongue spread in the floods,
dance of the heavy stream.

I lay across the abdomen of her purring pond;
I listen to the crackle of both branch and slapping rain.

I wander the woods as night fell away, heavy slumber
tugged at my eyes.

Well into the breach of morning, I plucked the jade colored
grass.

Softly, I burrow to the green glimpse of her eyes.
The passions of her flesh riddled along each measure
of moaning breath and quivering dew.

Host

I open my palms to the passions of the rain.
I unravel to the brine of the pulsing bay;
tenderly, I gather the droplets as the sky disrobes.

Kelp, trembling with the soothing waves,
I saunter to the heavy coast unto the heavy coast.

The malt of the greatest of all oceans
wraps me in coral which reaches beneath me
and dances as the swaggering seagull.

I gather the moisture of this slicing rain.
Turning my face to the delving sun, I pursue.

I quake beneath the weight of the sky.
I can hear the cry of the lighthouse as each sun
threads in every slippery host.

Soils Fade

To the soil I surrender my probing legs.
I dance to the flickering light of each flickering leaf.

Tender fog wraps as a robe upon my torso and neck.
I gesture my fingers into the deep of this stretching cotton.

I count the numbers of each blade of grass
As I watch the dew slip along each curving vein.

~

Into the threads of the crimping sunshine,
I wallow among each soothing pulse.

Gently, I turn to you and offer each crumbling dash of soil.
Along the stretching arrows of day, I turn to you and fade.

Trembling Dances

I enter the thicket of the heavy wood.
I loafe among the Autumn leaves and soothe
into the moaning ferns.

Into the darkest spot where the mosses lean,
I soaked through the smash of the burning sun;
I drizzle the creams of the approaching night.

Rising, I walk to the spread of the trembling river.
I drink heavily and turn to the silver threads of the moon.

Hearing your laughter which rumbles in the clatter
where branches dance, I walk to you in gentle night.

Earth Crumbles

Pinks dripped across the horizon as the softest purples
weaved a field of cotton.

I stand and face the death of the sun.
Revolving through the groaning sky,

I place myself upon the gentle bed of
ferns, lavender and lilacs.

~

The earth crumbles beneath me and I sulk
upon each eager fleece where the mosses sing
of the marrow of the dead.

I turn to you and offer myself to the
sweat of moaning nightfall.

Yoke of the Sky

Deepend from the sour snows of the south,
I stand and feel the dash of the winds
which strike in multitudes and open as a Winter harvest.

I gaze to the northern mountains.
Rocky gestures of hope pierce the thin breath of the sky.

Opening my lungs to this stroke of heavy night,
I coil through each prism of the sulking dome.

The sun, soft as yoke, blooms the threads
of this trembling Winter.

Evergreen Woods

The length of my shadow fell across the tamped leaves
and spread into the cloak of a deeper night.

I wrap myself across myself and burrow as a shroud.

Placing the oak leaf in my palm, I shred this page of night
into the flickering arms of each bush and shrub.

I look to the misty sky and shudder
beneath the crescent moon.

Dripping hours of approaching daylight,
I humble to the threads
of fog which sulk about me in tender kisses.

I dance to the arrows of meadow hosting the trembling trees.

Moments later, the soaking mask of
this burning sun weakens me
as I travel west to the evergreen woods.

Searching through a Moaning Wood

I listen to the crackling wings of the crow.
Feeling the burlap of the thicket and thornbush,
I slip through the gnarled woods.

The humid breath of the falling sky,
I probe the reaching trail;
quietly, the lilacs mumbled soft verbs to me as I passed.

From forest to pasture and distant meadow,
the earth tugs the step of my boots;
I whimper to the soothing navies of the morning horizon.

I lean against the willow tree and tread.
Every molecule of the forest moans to me in quiet dampness.

Calendar of Youth

I soothe across the freckled skin of your sloping chest.

With a moan, you quiver before me,
I soften my lips to the press of the loft of your garments.

I kneel. I swab the tensions of both abdomen and waist.

~

The heavy sun of the morning hour, I wade beneath you.
You stroke through my gentle hair and pulse against the crisp
dirt which humbles my feet and aching legs.

~

You brand as the calendar of my youth.
When I smell the lilies of your breath,

I sink to the earth and moan for your phantom flesh.

Walking in the Hour of Morning

The glaze of Summer slipped upon you.
Quietly, I lay so near to the moist
breath of your tender mouth.

Against the softest slope of your trembling waist,
aromas sulk past as the dewy morning
sheds along your quivering abdomen.

I open to the endless grains of wheat.
Together, we walk the fields and I reach my fingers
against the slick palms of your hands.

I shake the quivering arms of the elm as I pass
the patch of trees. Sweetly they cast shade upon us.

Maps

I read the lines of the ancient bark.
I learned the stories of my Father and his Father.

Patiently, I threaded my fingers across the heavy trunk.
Voices soft spoke to my eager ear.

~

In the blitz of morning, I smelled the ode dripping in sap.

~

Now, resting in the cloak of my bed,
a forgotten slumber falls upon me.

I sweat beneath each linen and blanket.
The song of the mourning dove keeps me lucid.

~

I close my eyes and through the forest I drift.

Morning Rhythms

I fracture the silence of night.
The songbird lulls to sleep.

Slowly, sweetly I speak to the motionless pond.
I awake to the green kelp as it fondles my feet.

~

In a cascade, I swim in the gestures of each morning rhythm.

~

An hour later, I am surrounded in the nearby woodlands.
Leaves graze upon my feet.

Oak Leaf

The river suckled the virgin soil,
slap of the tender muds surrendered beneath
my feet and heavy boots.

I drank from the white capped water and listened
to the foams as they trembled before me.

Chiseled, the northern mountain sank
springs and the thinnest misty air;
sitting by the edge of the fattened, boastful river,
I could hear the moans of my elders
as the single oak leaf wandered past.

Fragments

I press my way through the trembling Autumn breeze.
Curling leaves sulk beneath me as the great
oak mourns it's solitude in the distant fields of jade and
emerald grasses.

I seek the threading waters of the spiny dancing stream.
alone in this clamoring dust, I stand silent and lost.

Fragments of the flickering moon
shudder across each bantering branch,
so tender the mosses offer their delicate, soft soil.

I return to the heavy oak.
Sweetly, I sit on gnarled root and sheets of bark.

Vacating

Gently, her lips, breath, and tongue purred across as sweet
verbs drizzling in hunger.

Quietly, I removed the cottons which crawled along,
soothed in milks.

I coveted the humid glaze which grew slippery
upon the near, quaking window.

In the crimp of her softest gasp, I
shook along her tender side,
flank of the throbbing heart.

Shadows drawn from the candle flame, I floundered
my sight upon ceiling and each bead of wax.

~

Now, the grasp of morning chiseled it's way from silks
to the tremors of a wailing breeze, shouting across the room.

~

I felt a softness on the press of my feet as I
swept through the garden grass.

By the fountain, I watched her standing gently
before the window and all it's groaning tales.

When Fog Falls

Into the dash of night, I watched her disrobe before the cool,
trembling rings of the moon.

Quickly with surrender, I wrapped into the coiling grip
of her soft, heavy arms; the press of her
tender breasts awakened through the lavender sky.

A surmounting warmth rose from the powdered glaze
of her flickering thighs.

~

Fog dripped, depressed along the silk moisture
covering her nakedness.

Shadows crawling across these grasses,
plants, and scattered trees,
I awaited the mist to rise and sweetly
touched her pale, creamy
arms as each thread of cotton rose to the sauntering treetops.

~

Gingerly, I swabbed in the hymns of her sultry voice.

I fell back, walking through the wet
spears of each grassy patch.

Soon, you became lost to me.

Wading before the Moon

The cool water tugged as a shroud.
I soothed into the bay and felt the kelp stroke me
as the sauces of a foreign, dripping cloak
which swabbed across my legs and welcomed my feet.

Distant, the lighthouse danced each probe of light.
I heard the moaning boats tremble across the heavy gap.

Returning to shore, the pebbles and soil
held me as the froth of the water, suckled from the bay,
clinging to my legs.

I turned to the proud grip of the moon.
I listened to her voice upon the sulking wind.

Vanilla and Sandalwood

I touched you softly as the fall of webbing mist
which threads upon the gentle flesh you
so quietly display, triumph of a falling dress.

Soils gather as mud while I walk through each
suckle of my toes and heels.

I think of you as you fade into moonlight.
I smell the fragrances you carry with you,

Heavy vanilla and a grip of sandalwood
linger for a moment, then gone.

~

Returning to this place, each day, each year,
I tremble about the snapping arms of twilight.

I can hear the shouts of the dead as I walk through
the tender lisp of the falling rain.

Into the softness of you, I sleep upon
this eager pouch of grass.

Awake in the Arms of Night

I stood so close to the dwarf weeping cherry tree,
I trembled to the touch of each blossom as they soothed
the silent dance of my glaze covered flesh.

The moon glanced through the trees as I watched
this sliver of silver burrow through the branches and petals
which fell in abundance to the rocky, moss covered earth.

Walking through this garden and humble grotto,
I wandered along with the proud display of each spice
and the grip of the scouring wind as it danced along my hair.

I drift among the crowned patch of weeds.
I return to the down pillow which molded to the warm
press of my cheek and roamed along each fiber of each tree
and gripping shrub and bush.

Drinking from the Mountain Spring

The dusty dirt path rose into the curve
of the woods which led to the mountain,
gripped to the earth upon its haunches.

I passed the pine, I passed the maple;
quietly, I knelt to the fern which observed me in leaf
and stem.

I searched the forested hills.
Looking for a trickling source of water
as the stream bent and dragged.

As the day dripped into night,
I glanced upon the bleeding navy and pink trim of the sky.

I lay by the bank of the flushing stream.
Quickly, I snatched a piece of driftwood;
water pulsed across ripples and jagged rocks.

By morning, the thinnest of air shrouded across
the mountain peak.

Here, I drank heavy.

Velvets and the Bursting Pod

Wild flowers danced to the wind which covered the all the forests of all the earth.
Walking the woodland floor, I sweetly tasted the pollens as they bloomed from each growing pod.

Green velvet mosses caked the rock laden road as I hiked to the summit where the orchid suckled the sunshine.

Warmth in Slumber as I Dream by Riverside

I slipped my hands into the pouch of life.
Each finger danced on this heavy, powdered dough.
Silent, I slept warmly by the river;

With the first hour of morning,
I watched the dusts of the earth flicker across the sky.

About the Author

Donny Barilla, a poet covering the realms: human intimacy, nature, mythology, theology, and man's relationship with death and the departed, has been writing for over three decades. He writes daily and strives to renew himself as an artist from page to page and body of work to body of work. Very seldom does he take a break from writing as he views it as a full-time job. He lives a reclusive lifestyle and finds himself clinging close to nature and all her elements. His home state of Pennsylvania strikes chords of poetic depth about him as he finds loveliness from cornfield to meadow. Whether it's feelings of love, intimacy, or a special closeness, he maintains the feeling that death does not take these with him/her to the grave. Emotions and feeling outlast the flesh of the human body. Human intimacy draws near an enigmatic spiritual passion which conquers all on the prismatic scale of experience. When speaking of mythology Donny says, "myths were created to make sense of feelings which are complicated by very nature. They are perhaps more easily understood through persons greater than oneself. As for theology, a disciplined aspect, incorporates quite finely with passions and secured poetic comforts.

https://twitter.com/BarillaDonny

www.ingramcontent.com/pod-product-compliance
Lightning Source LLC
Chambersburg PA
CBHW032226080426
42735CB00008B/735